PROGRAMMING EXPERIMENTS IN NEURAL NETWORKS IN C + +

PROGRAMMING EXPERIMENTS IN NEURAL NETWORKS IN C + +

Skrevet av Christopher Bertram,

San Francisco, Ca.

Analoge data Enterprises, San Francisco, Ca.

PROGRAMMING EXPERIMENTS IN NEURAL NETWORKS IN C + +

Richard Feynman, Feynman Lectures on Computation, 1970

[Datamaskiner] utvikler seg så raskt at selv dataforskere ikke kan holde tritt med dem. Det må være forvirrende for de fleste matematikere og ingeniører ... Til tross for mangfoldet av søknadene, metodene for å angripe vanskelige problemer med datamaskiner viser en stor enhet, og navnet Computer Sciences blir festet til disiplin som det framgår . Det må imidlertid forstås at dette fremdeles er et felt som i sin struktur er fremdeles uklare. Studenten vil finne svært mange flere problemer enn svar.

Innholdsfortegnelse

Liste over illustrasjoner

Innledning

Dette prosjektet ble skrevet i C + + v.11, med Microsoft Visual Studio 2013.

Bidragsytere til denne boken

Christopher D. Bertram

Chapter 1

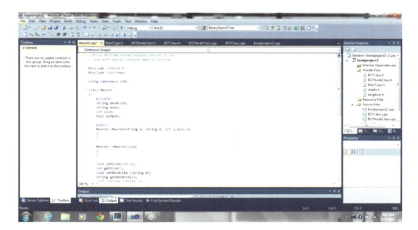

Figure 1. I dette bildet: Forfatteren bringer opp filene etter at en konsoll prosjekt av filene som er inkludert i neste kapittel. Filene kompilere å danne en konsoll applikasjon, og en kjørbar som kan løpe uavhengig av hverandre.

Abstrakt

Neural nettverk har vært med oss i lang tid, i kunstig intelligens (Newell, Shaw, Simon, 1956). Koblede Listen brukes i alt fra Word Processing til database design, men: de problemene nå står overfor brukerne er minnelekkasjer og kompromisser til sikkerhet. Novel implementering av binært søketre og den nyeste kompilatoren kan løse disse spørsmål om sikkerhet i en vitenskap som startet som modeller av det menneskelige sinn.

1. Selv om det aldri kan være en sann identitet tilstand mellom sinn og hjerne heretter sinnet kropp reduksjon (Searle, 1985), kan Neural Networks være konstruert for å operere som modeller av nerveceller. Her vil jeg presentere et binært søketre implementering som gren som nerveceller. Mens noen binært søketre er rett og slett en lenket liste brukket i to; Binary søketre presenteres her fungerer på en annen måte.

2. Det er en multi-aksial Binary etter treet gjennomføring her som har et formål å illustrere punkt faktiske biologiske cellefunksjon. Ved å gjøre det, og bryte med tradisjonelle definisjoner av lenket liste, og binært søketre, har det vist seg å være svært nyttig.

3. Den versjonen av Microsoft Visual Studio som implementerer de nyeste reglene for C + + faktisk gir de hjelp av lekkasjefrie programmering hvis smartpekersystemet brukes til lenkede lister og Binary Search Trees. Mens det er mulig å benytte større pekere det er den nye markøren system som gir lekkasjefritt gjennomføring. Det er med lekkasjen gratis pekeren gjennomføring her, og romanen binært søketre som gir den sikkerheten som trengs i den fiendtlige miljø som brukerne i dag finne seg inn i å.

4. Basen Node av romanen binært søketre som presenteres her er et objekt kalt Neuron. Den Neuron her har inngangsverdien, og utgangsverdien, samt en beslutningsverdi, som er boolsk. Dette kan være nyttig på en rekke måter, for eksempel et andre språk ordboken, men i forbindelse med diskusjonen har bare vært brukt for demonstrasjonsformål . Ved å gjøre dette er

hele demonstrasjonen romanen og tjener formålet for illustrasjon for den sanne nevrale nettverk purist.

5. Den endelige krypterings bruk kan betjenes fra en gitt implementering som diskutert i det følgende. I substitusjon cypher messaging ett ord brukes for et annet ord, og så thusly; i Neuron av den gitte gjennomføringen én verdi er en inngang ord og en annen verdi er utgangs ord: substitusjon ordet er gitt i produksjonen av hver Neuron i binært søketre, og så videre thusly: opererer som et grensesnitt mellom den konfidensielle data og substitusjon cypher nøkkelen, romanen binært søketre fungerer som den ultimate sikkerhetsprogramvare både som Leak Gratis system, og den sterkeste krypteringssystemet mulig.

6. I et eksempel på hvordan et slikt sikkerhetssystem kunne brukes, kunne et ord liste over substantiver erstattes av en annen i en tekstbehandler og en sikker melding kunne bli skrevet. Når skrives ut, vil meldingen vises i en form som kan være relatert mens i virkeligheten meldingen kan inneholde et helt annen betydning når dekodet.

7. Mens faktisk eksempel ikke inneholder en cypher substitusjon system, en metode som tillater det, kan det bli konstruert. For å gjøre det ville man lage et objekt som leser i byttelisten og plasserer ordet listen i binært søketre ved å bruke Set-funksjonen. Neste skritt vil være å opprette utskriftsfunksjonen som ville gi en liste over ord som vil bli skrevet ut for hvert ord i ordlisten når de skrives ut. Med binært søketre lastet en annen struktur i en tekstbehandler ville bruke en lenket liste over objekter hvor en teksteditor ville virkelig være en lenket liste over objekter. I en hypotetisk cypher substitusjon system operatør ville bare skrive en melding, og ville ikke trenger å være klar over hvordan eller hva meldingen vil si når de skrives ut, og heller ikke ville mottakeren av en melding engang trenger å være klar over hva inngangs meldingen inneholdt . Det kan være en sømløs cypher substitusjon system meldinger implementert ved ganske enkelt å endre eksempel.

Konklusjon

En ny implementering av et nevralt nettverk er presentert her som i det lekkasjefrie omgivelser av den siste C + + sammenstilling kan brukes som det endelige kryptering verktøy i substitusjons cypher systemer. Romanen eksempel er en illustrasjon av hvordan hjernen fungerer mens læring i forgrening nervøse vev.

Chapter 2

Eksperiment: Lag en type Neural nettverket som beskrevet i kapittel

Purister vil fortelle deg, selv på fester på tre om morgenen at Neural Networks er spesielle ting med ulike regler og ulike typer. De er strukturer av en proveniens dypt i informatikk antikken. Du kan ikke ta disse klassene som en førsteårsstudent, etc.

Så da med øl i hånden Jeg har alltid hevdet at det bør være et nettverk som hadde et objekt - en Neuron som kunne grenen ut som å lære Nerveceller i noen ens hode.

Så da går ned i kaninhullet av en slik innsats er det faktisk noe nytt. Hvem visste at nettopp det ville være å gjøre det hele om igjen fra scratch?

Så for å sikkerhetskopiere sa kapittelet jeg måtte skrive min egen. Her er da min versjon av et nettverk. Koden purister vil gå over dette med en fin tann kam. Det finnes to versjoner inkludert og de kompilere uten feil. De er demonstrasjoner. De kan bli endret for din søknad. Frem til nå noe programvare som er skrevet på alle språk hadde minnelekkasjer. Disse versjonene spesielt Microsoft 2013 har svært lite, om noe minnelekkasjer.

Det bør være åtte tekstfiler i prosjektet (for hver versjon).

There should be 8 text files in the project (for each version).

Program.cpp

UserMenu.cpp

Neuron.cpp

TreeFormatter.cpp

UserMenu.h

Neuron.h

TreeFormatter.h

BinarySearchTree.h

This project was written in C++ v.11, with Microsoft Visual Studio 2013.

```cpp
// programm.cpp : Defines the entry point for the console application.
// MSVS 2013

#include "UserMenu.h"
#include <iostream>
#include <cstdlib>
#include <fstream>
#include <string>

void main()
{
    CUserMenu().ProcessUserInput();
}
```

```cpp
// Neuron.h : Header File For Neuron.cpp.
// MSVS 2013


#pragma once

#include <string>
#include <iostream>

class CNeuron
{
public:
        friend std::ostream& operator << (std::ostream& os, const CNeuron& item);
        friend std::ostream& operator << (std::ostream& os, const CNeuron* item);

        CNeuron(
                const std::string& dendrite,
                const std::string& axon,
                const int size,
                const bool output) :
                        m_dendrite(dendrite),
                        m_axon(axon),
                        m_size(size),
                        m_output(output)
        {
        }

        const std::string& GetKey() const { return m_dendrite; };

        const std::string& GetDendrite() const { return m_dendrite; };

        const std::string& GetAxon() const { return m_axon; };

        const bool AxonHillock() const { return m_output; };

        const int GetSize() const { return m_size; };
```

```cpp
private:

        CNeuron& operator = (const CNeuron&) {};


        const std::string m_dendrite;


        const std::string m_axon;


        const bool m_output;


        const int m_size;
};


std::ostream& operator << (std::ostream& os, const CNeuron& item);
std::ostream& operator << (std::ostream& os, const CNeuron* item);
```

```cpp
// Neuron.cpp
// MSVS 2013


#include "Neuron.h"

std::ostream& operator << (std::ostream& os, const CNeuron& item)
{
       return os
              << "[ Dendrit: '" << item.m_dendrite
              << "', Axon: '" << item.m_axon
              << "', Size: " << item.m_size
              << ", AxonHillock: " << (item.m_output ? "yes" : "no")
              << " ]";
}


std::ostream& operator << (std::ostream& os, const CNeuron* item)
{
       return os << *(item);
}
```

```cpp
// UserMenu.cpp
// MSVS 2013

#include "UserMenu.h"

#include "BinarySearchTree.h"
#include "Neuron.h"

#include "TreeFormatter.h"

#include <string>
#include <iostream>

namespace
{

int printMenuHeaderAndAskUser()
{
    int choice = 0;
    std::cout << "\n\n"
        << " --------------------- \n"
        << " 1. Insertion/Creation \n"
        << " 2. In-Order Traversal \n"
        << " 3. Pre-Order Traversal \n"
        << " 4. Post-Order Traversal \n"
        << " 5. Find and Print \n"
        << " 6. Find and Remove \n"
        << " 7. Exit \n"
        << " --------------------- \n"
        << " Enter your choice : ";

    std::cin >> choice;

    if (std::cin.fail())
    {
        std::cin.clear();
        std::cin.ignore(std::numeric_limits<std::streamsize>::max(), '\n');
    }
```

```cpp
        return choice;
}


template<typename T>
const T askUserAboutNamedValue(const std::string& key)
{
        T value;
        std::cout << "Enter " << key << " value for node: ";
        std::cin >> value;
        return value;
}


void printNodeValue(const CNeuron* item)
{
        if (item == nullptr)
        {
                std::cout << "Key not found. Try again, please." << std::endl;
        }
        else
        {
                std::cout << "Find result: " << item << std::endl;
        }


}


CUserMenu::CUserMenu(void) :
        m_tree(new CTree())
{
}


CUserMenu::~CUserMenu(void)
{
}


void CUserMenu::ProcessUserInput(void)
{
```

```cpp
std::cout << " -- Valley Process Software Menu -- " << std::endl;

int choice = 0;
while (choice != 7)
{
    int choice = printMenuHeaderAndAskUser();
    switch (choice)
    {
    case 1:
        {
            auto dendrite = askUserAboutNamedValue<std::string>("dendrite");
            auto axon = askUserAboutNamedValue<std::string>("axon");
            auto size = askUserAboutNamedValue<int>("size");
            m_tree->Insert(CNeuron(dendrite, axon, size, true));
        }
        break;
    case 2:
        CTreeFormatter().PrintInOrder(*(m_tree.get()));
        break;
    case 3:
        CTreeFormatter().PrintPreOrder(*(m_tree.get()));
        break;
    case 4:
        CTreeFormatter().PrintPostOrder(*(m_tree.get()));
        break;
    case 5:
        {
            auto key = askUserAboutNamedValue<std::string>("dendrite");
            auto node = m_tree->Find(key);
            printNodeValue(node);
        }
        break;
    case 6:
        {
            auto key = askUserAboutNamedValue<std::string>("dendrite");
            m_tree->Remove(key);
        }
        break;
```

```
            }
        }
    }
```

```cpp
// UserMenu.h
// MSVS 2013

#pragma once

#include <string>
#include <memory>

class CNeuron;
template<typename TItem, typename TKey> class CBinarySearchTree;

class CUserMenu
{
public:
    CUserMenu(void);
    ~CUserMenu(void);

    void ProcessUserInput(void);

private:
    typedef CBinarySearchTree<CNeuron, std::string> CTree;
    const std::unique_ptr<CTree> m_tree;
};
```

```cpp
// BinarySearchTree.h
// MSVS 2013



#pragma once

#include <memory>

template<typename TItem, typename TKey>
class CBinarySearchTree
{
public:
        friend class CTreeFormatter;

        CBinarySearchTree(void) :
                m_root(nullptr),
                m_size(0)
        {};

        ~CBinarySearchTree(void) {};

        int GetSize(void) const { return m_size; }

        bool IsEmpty(void) const { return GetSize() == 0; }

        void Insert(const TItem& item)
        {
                insert(item, m_root);
        }

        void Remove(const TKey& key)
        {
                remove(key, m_root);
        }

        TItem* Find(const TKey& key) const
        {
```

```cpp
            return find(key, m_root);
        }


private:
        class CNode;
        typedef std::unique_ptr<CNode> CNodePtr;
        typedef std::unique_ptr<TItem> TItemPtr;


        class CNode
        {
        public:
                CNode(const TItem& item) :
                        m_item(new TItem(item)),
                        m_left(nullptr),
                        m_right(nullptr)
                {};


                int CompareTo(const TItem& item) const { return CompareTo(item.GetKey()); }


                int CompareTo(const TKey& key) const { return m_item->GetKey().compare(key); }


                TItemPtr m_item;


                CNodePtr m_left;


                CNodePtr m_right;
        };


        void insert(const TItem& item, CNodePtr& node)
        {
                if (!node)
                {
                        node.reset(new CNode(item));
                        ++m_size;
                        return;
                }


                auto compare = node->CompareTo(item);
```

```cpp
            if (compare < 0)

            {

                    insert(item, node->m_right);

            }

            else

            {

                    insert(item, node->m_left);

            }

    }


TItem* find(const TKey& key, const CNodePtr& node) const

    {

            if (!node)

            {

                    return nullptr;

            }


            auto compare = node->CompareTo(key);

            if (compare == 0)

            {

                    return node->m_item.get();

            }

            else if (compare < 0)

            {

                    return find(key, node->m_right);

            }

            else

            {

                    return find(key, node->m_left);

            }

    }


    void remove (const TKey& key, CNodePtr& node)

    {

            if (!node)

            {

                    return;

            }
```

```cpp
auto compare = node->CompareTo(key);
if (compare == 0)
{
    if (node->m_left != nullptr && node->m_right != nullptr)
    {
        auto& rightLeft = node->m_right->m_left;
        if (rightLeft.get() == nullptr)
        {
            rightLeft = std::move(node->m_left);
            node = std::move(node->m_right);
        }
        else
        {
            node->m_item = std::move(rightLeft->m_item);
            remove(node->m_item->GetKey(), rightLeft);
            return;
        }
    }
    else if (node->m_left != nullptr)
    {
        node = std::move(node->m_left);
    }
    else if (node->m_right != nullptr)
    {
        node = std::move(node->m_right);
    }
    else
    {
        node.release();
    }

    --m_size;
}
else if (compare < 0)
{
    remove(key, node->m_right);
}
```

```cpp
        else
        {
                remove(key, node->m_left);
        }
    }
}

    CNodePtr m_root;

    int m_size;
};
```

```cpp
// TreeFormatter.cpp
// MSVS 2013

#include "TreeFormatter.h"

#include <iostream>

void CTreeFormatter::printInOrder(const CTree::CNodePtr& node)
{
        if (node.get() == nullptr)
        {
                return;
        }

        printInOrder(node->m_left);
        std::cout << node->m_item.get() << std::endl;
        printInOrder(node->m_right);
}

void CTreeFormatter::printPreOrder(const CTree::CNodePtr& node)
{
        if (node.get() == nullptr)
        {
                return;
        }

        std::cout << node->m_item.get() << std::endl;
        printPreOrder(node->m_left);
        printPreOrder(node->m_right);
}

void CTreeFormatter::printPostOrder(const CTree::CNodePtr& node)
{
        if (node.get() == nullptr)
        {
                return;
        }
```

```
    printPostOrder(node->m_left);

    printPostOrder(node->m_right);

    std::cout << node->m_item.get() << std::endl;

}
```

```cpp
// TreeFormatter.h
// MSVS 2013


#pragma once

#include "BinarySearchTree.h"
#include "Neuron.h"

#include <string>

class CTreeFormatter
{
public:
        typedef CBinarySearchTree<CNeuron, std::string> CTree;

        void PrintInOrder(const CTree& tree) const { printInOrder(tree.m_root); }
        void PrintPreOrder(const CTree& tree) const { printPreOrder(tree.m_root); }
        void PrintPostOrder(const CTree& tree) const { printPostOrder(tree.m_root); };

private:
        static void printInOrder(const CTree::CNodePtr& node);
        static void printPreOrder(const CTree::CNodePtr& node);
        static void printPostOrder(const CTree::CNodePtr& node);
};
```

```cpp
// programm.cpp : Defines the entry point for the console application.
// MSVS 2010

#include "UserMenu.h"

int main(int argc, char* argv[])
{
    CUserMenu().ProcessUserInput();

    return 0;
}
```

```cpp
// Neuron.cpp MSVS 2010


#include "Neuron.h"


std::ostream& operator << (std::ostream& os, const CNeuron& item)
{
    return os
        << "[ Dendrit: '" << item.m_dendrite
        << "', Axon: '" << item.m_axon
        << "', Size: " << item.m_size
        << ", AxonHillock: " << (item.m_output ? "yes" : "no")
        << " ]";
}


std::ostream& operator << (std::ostream& os, const CNeuron* item)
{
    return os << *(item);
}
```

```cpp
// Neuron.h MSVS 2010


#pragma once


#include <string>
#include <iostream>


class CNeuron
{
public:
        friend std::ostream& operator << (std::ostream& os, const CNeuron& item);
        friend std::ostream& operator << (std::ostream& os, const CNeuron* item);


        CNeuron(
                const std::string& dendrite,
                const std::string& axon,
                const int size,
                const bool output) :
                        m_dendrite(dendrite),
                        m_axon(axon),
                        m_size(size),
                        m_output(output)
        {
        }


        const std::string& GetKey() const { return m_dendrite; };


        const std::string& GetDendrite() const { return m_dendrite; };


        const std::string& GetAxon() const { return m_axon; };


        const bool AxonHillock() const { return m_output; };


        const int GetSize() const { return m_size; };

private:
        const std::string m_dendrite;
```

```cpp
        const std::string m_axon;

        const bool m_output;

        const int m_size;
};


std::ostream& operator << (std::ostream& os, const CNeuron& item);
std::ostream& operator << (std::ostream& os, const CNeuron* item);
```

```cpp
// UserMenu.cpp MSVS 2010

#include "UserMenu.h"

#include "BinarySearchTree.h"
#include "Neuron.h"

#include "TreeFormatter.h"

#include <string>
#include <iostream>

namespace
{

int printMenuHeaderAndAskUser()
{
    int choice = 0;
    std::cout << "\n\n"
        << " ---------------------- \n"
        << " 1. Insertion/Creation \n"
        << " 2. In-Order Traversal \n"
        << " 3. Pre-Order Traversal \n"
        << " 4. Post-Order Traversal \n"
        << " 5. Find and Print \n"
        << " 6. Find and Remove \n"
        << " 7. Exit \n"
        << " ---------------------- \n"
        << " Enter your choice : ";

    std::cin >> choice;

    if (std::cin.fail())
    {
        std::cin.clear();
        std::cin.ignore(std::numeric_limits<std::streamsize>::max(), '\n');
    }
```

```cpp
        return choice;

}


template<typename T>
const T askUserAboutNamedValue(const std::string& key)
{
        T value;
        std::cout << "Enter " << key << " value for node: ";
        std::cin >> value;
        return value;
}


void printNodeValue(const CNeuron* item)
{
        if (item == nullptr)
        {
                std::cout << "Key not found. Try again, please." << std::endl;
        }
        else
        {
                std::cout << "Find result: " << item << std::endl;
        }

}


CUserMenu::CUserMenu(void) :
        m_tree(new CTree())
{
}


CUserMenu::~CUserMenu(void)
{
}


void CUserMenu::ProcessUserInput(void)
{
        std::cout << " -- Valley Process Software Menu -- " << std::endl;
```

```cpp
while(true)
{
    int choice = printMenuHeaderAndAskUser();
    switch (choice)
    {
    case 1:
        {
            auto dendrite = askUserAboutNamedValue<std::string>("dendrite");
            auto axon = askUserAboutNamedValue<std::string>("axon");
            auto size = askUserAboutNamedValue<int>("size");
            m_tree->Insert(CNeuron(dendrite, axon, size, true));
        }
        break;
    case 2:
        CTreeFormatter().PrintInOrder(*(m_tree.get()));
        break;
    case 3:
        CTreeFormatter().PrintPreOrder(*(m_tree.get()));
        break;
    case 4:
        CTreeFormatter().PrintPostOrder(*(m_tree.get()));
        break;
    case 5:
        {
            auto key = askUserAboutNamedValue<std::string>("dendrite");
            auto node = m_tree->Find(key);
            printNodeValue(node);
        }
        break;
    case 6:
        {
            auto key = askUserAboutNamedValue<std::string>("dendrite");
            m_tree->Remove(key);
        }
        break;
    case 7:
        return;
```

```
        default:
            break;
    }
}
}
```

```cpp
// UserMenu.h MSVS 2010


#pragma once


#include <string>
#include <memory>


class CNeuron;
template<typename TItem, typename TKey> class CBinarySearchTree;


class CUserMenu
{
public:
    CUserMenu(void);
    ~CUserMenu(void);


    void ProcessUserInput(void);

private:
    typedef CBinarySearchTree<CNeuron, std::string> CTree;
    const std::unique_ptr<CTree> m_tree;
};
```

```cpp
// BinarySearchTree.h MSVS

#pragma once

#include <memory>

class CTreeFormatter;

template<typename TItem, typename TKey>
class CBinarySearchTree
{
public:
        friend class CTreeFormatter;

        CBinarySearchTree(void) :
                m_root(nullptr),
                m_size(0)
        {};

        ~CBinarySearchTree(void) {};

        int GetSize(void) const { return m_size; }

        bool IsEmpty(void) const { return GetSize() == 0; }

        void Insert(const TItem& item)
        {
                insert(item, m_root);
        }

        void Remove(const TKey& key)
        {
                remove(key, m_root);
        }

        TItem* Find(const TKey& key) const
        {
                return find(key, m_root);
```

```cpp
        }

private:
        class CNode;

#if _MSC_VER == 1600
        struct CNodeDeleter
        {
                void operator()(CNode* ptr) { delete ptr; }
        };

        typedef std::unique_ptr<CNode, CNodeDeleter> CNodePtr;
#else
        typedef std::unique_ptr<CNode> CNodePtr;
#endif

        typedef std::unique_ptr<TItem> TItemPtr;

        class CNode
        {
        public:
                CNode(const TItem& item) :
                        m_item(new TItem(item)),
                        m_left(nullptr),
                        m_right(nullptr)
                {
                };

                int CompareTo(const TItem& item) const { return CompareTo(item.GetKey()); }

                int CompareTo(const TKey& key) const { return m_item->GetKey().compare(key); }

                TItemPtr m_item;

                CNodePtr m_left;

                CNodePtr m_right;
        };
```

```cpp
void insert(const TItem& item, CNodePtr& node)
{
        if (node.get() == nullptr)
        {
                node.reset(new CNode(item));
                ++m_size;
                return;
        }

        auto compare = node->CompareTo(item);
        if (compare < 0)
        {
                insert(item, node->m_right);
        }
        else
        {
                insert(item, node->m_left);
        }
}

TItem* find(const TKey& key, const CNodePtr& node) const
{
        if (node.get() == nullptr)
        {
                return nullptr;
        }

        auto compare = node->CompareTo(key);
        if (compare == 0)
        {
                return node->m_item.get();
        }
        else if (compare < 0)
        {
                return find(key, node->m_right);
        }
        else
```

```cpp
        {
            return find(key, node->m_left);
        }
    }
}


void remove (const TKey& key, CNodePtr& node)
{
    if (node.get() == nullptr)
    {
        return;
    }

    auto compare = node->CompareTo(key);
    if (compare == 0)
    {
        if (node->m_left != nullptr && node->m_right != nullptr)
        {
            if (node->m_right->m_left.get() == nullptr)
            {
                node->m_right->m_left = std::move(node->m_left);
                node = std::move(node->m_right);
            }
            else
            {
                node->m_item = std::move(node->m_right->m_left->m_item);
                remove(node->m_item->GetKey(), node->m_right->m_left);
                return;
            }
        }
        else if (node->m_left != nullptr)
        {
            node = std::move(node->m_left);
        }
        else if (node->m_right != nullptr)
        {
            node = std::move(node->m_right);
        }
        else
```

```cpp
            {
                    node.release();
            }


            --m_size;
        }
        else if (compare < 0)
        {
                remove(key, node->m_right);
        }
        else
        {
                remove(key, node->m_left);
        }
    }


    CNodePtr m_root;


    int m_size;
};
```

```cpp
// TreeFormatter.cpp MSVS 2010


#include "TreeFormatter.h"

#include <iostream>

void CTreeFormatter::printInOrder(const CTree::CNodePtr& node)
{
        if (node.get() == nullptr)
        {
                return;
        }


        printInOrder(node->m_left);
        std::cout << node->m_item.get() << std::endl;
        printInOrder(node->m_right);
}


void CTreeFormatter::printPreOrder(const CTree::CNodePtr& node)
{
        if (node.get() == nullptr)
        {
                return;
        }


        std::cout << node->m_item.get() << std::endl;
        printPreOrder(node->m_left);
        printPreOrder(node->m_right);
}


void CTreeFormatter::printPostOrder(const CTree::CNodePtr& node)
{
        if (node.get() == nullptr)
        {
                return;
        }
```

```cpp
    printPostOrder(node->m_left);
    printPostOrder(node->m_right);
    std::cout << node->m_item.get() << std::endl;
}
```

```cpp
// TreeFormatter.h MSVS 2010

#pragma once

#include "BinarySearchTree.h"
#include "Neuron.h"

#include <string>

class CTreeFormatter
{
public:
        typedef CBinarySearchTree<CNeuron, std::string> CTree;

        void PrintInOrder(const CTree& tree) const { printInOrder(tree.m_root); }
        void PrintPreOrder(const CTree& tree) const { printPreOrder(tree.m_root); }
        void PrintPostOrder(const CTree& tree) const { printPostOrder(tree.m_root); };

private:
        static void printInOrder(const CTree::CNodePtr& node);
        static void printPreOrder(const CTree::CNodePtr& node);
        static void printPostOrder(const CTree::CNodePtr& node);
};
```

Appendix

Curriculum Vitae

UNIVERSITY OF CALIFORNIA, BERKELEY, Berkeley, California

Clinical Laboratory Scientist Preparatory Program *(Currently pursuing certificate in Clinical Laboratory Scientist Preparatory Program)*

SAN FRANCISCO STATE UNIVERSITY, San Francisco, California

Bachelor of Science in General Biology w/ Minor Computer Science

HEALD INSTITUTE OF TECHNOLOGY, San Francisco, California

Associate in Applied Science, Electronics & Networking Technology *(Dual Major)*

MERRITT COLLEGE, Oakland, California

Associate in Science, Math/ Natural Science & Associate in Art, Social and Behavioral Sciences *(Dual Major)*

AMERICAN RIVER COLLEGE, Carmichael, California

Associate in Science, General Science